Mind Diamonds
Shining on Your Mind

ISBN: 9780578732497

Book Categories: Poetry

Table of Contents

How Can I Be A Teacher Although I'm Still Learning

Every teacher has to get their knowledge
from another source
As students we just follow in their course
What we've learned from them
can then be taught to others
Handed down to younger siblings
from their sisters and brothers

Knowledge is meant to be passed on
Of our legacy this will be the greatest milestone
It isn't something that we should squander
In our archives should be lessons
that makes the mind ponder

I still have a lot to learn
In the process, millions of my brain cells will burn
While this is going on, I also have a lot to teach
There are thousands of people
that I want my knowledge to reach

Some people look for me to teach them a thing or two
I give them more lessons than a few
Teaching them also allows me to learn a lesson
Sharing our life experiences is a blessing

Every teacher has to be taught
In the web of learning we are caught
Knowledge is something
for which I'll always be yearning
I will teach others although I am still learning

Pushing Language To Its Limit

The writer attempts to take language as far as it can go
There seems to be no limit
to how they make the words flow
Creative beyond belief
even when writing about the imaginary
They leave sentences suspended in the air like gravity

For the writer, the page is empty like outer space
Allowing them to go wherever they please
on the universe's face
Writing is like matter in the life that revolves around it
Communication is music to our ears
with harmony at a perfect pitch

A language teacher was asked,
can language be taken to its limit and beyond
She said that it can be taken as far
as the mind can expound
You have to exercise muscles

that you've never used before
Lifting words from the depths of your psyche
until you can't find anymore

Choreograph the words so they can do a lyrical dance
Let them stand still long enough to make their stance
See how the sentences make their mind wonder
Mathematically written but yet not hard to solve
like a geometry number

Simple truths can be so well written
The pristine language will leave your mind smitten
The first thing that we learn
is writing and arithmetic's
We must take it to a higher level
and push language to its limits

What Will You Contribute To The World

When you pass away, what will you leave here
What words of yours will the people come to revere
This short life is only a brief segment
It's like being in the womb of the universe
before the hereafter was pregnant

We should all contribute something to this world
before we go
Let our descendants learn lessons
when they flip through our portfolio
At once upon a time,
we could have been a hell raiser
Hopefully by the time we depart,
we have turned into a trailblazer

The world is not just some big playground
There is serious work to be found
What will be the fulfillment of your life

Weigh the good and bad and see what's most rife

A lot of people avoid this topic
To them death is so catastrophic
Either way we will all face death
What's important is the legacy
of our mental and spiritual wealth

We must pass our wisdom to the next generation
Our contribution to the world
will be our demonstration
Human beings all started off as a boy or girl
When we die as adults
what will be our contribution to the world

THE MIGHTIEST TREE WAS ONCE A SEED

From a seed sprouted this mighty tree
If you know someone whose life is comparable
I want you to know that this is written in parable

The biggest things started off small
That tiny seed was the cause of it all
Once it was planted it grew its roots
To be the mightiest
was one of its earliest pursuits

How did it endure the winter once its leaves fell
Each branch has its own struggle to tell
The battle was always uphill
The sower of the seed had to till

In time this tree will get old

Its branches will bend and fold
Yet they still stand
Remaining an integral part of the land

Out of the dirt this seed rose
Growing into a tree
creating new life in its perpetual pose
Planted into an empty space
in the soil to fulfill a need
Looking at this mighty tree
is hard to believe it was once just a seed

WITHOUT FEAR OF REJECTION

You must face life without the fear of rejection
None of us will reach perfection
In life we all get turned down
Don't let fear stop you from trying
the next time around

Fear of rejection will only hold you back
Loosen up and give yourself some slack
Get courageous and fight your fear
Be strong because it will always be near

Hold your composure and maintain posture
Go down the list and check it off of the roster
It is just another human emotion

One that you should not give so much devotion

Do not shy away due to fear of a skeptic
Go after your dreams and do something epic
They said that nothing beats a failure but a try
So if you don't pursue the opportunity
then kiss it good-bye

For worry of fear your dreams you can abort
Before you even get started,
you'll give yourself a thwart
We must find things that fit us
and make our selection
Going through life without the fear of rejection

WISDOM FROM THE MOUTH OF BABIES

Everyday wisdom flows from the mouth of babies
They will grow into future gentleman and ladies
What I write is a true story and not some fable
Jesus spoke from the cradle

Wisdom can be gained from a child
This is not farfetched and wild
We need to listen to our kid
Stop dismissing their opinion
in a nonchalant bid

Let the children have their say

In the next generation they will control the day
The way they formulate their words
may not always be delightful
If you listen closely,
you'll discover they're very insightful

We refuse to listen to them
and that is why are children are rebelling
They have developed their own way
of story telling

It's a new form of language they have birthed
Therein is much wisdom to be unearthed

When babies talk they don't just babble
In order to understand their mode
of communication we should grapple

There is no ifs, ands, buts, or maybes
Wisdom does come forth
from the mouths of babies

AN IDEA WHOSE TIME HAS COME

Nothing can stop an idea whose time has come
History and nature pairs,
it with the person who will get the job done
All the odds in the world won't stop them
A revolutionary idea
is more precious than a gem

Inside the idea lives the entire blueprint
The brain that it enters
feels that it is heaven sent

Something epic is on the surface
Now this person has found their purpose

When it is time for it to happen,
it will take place
Moving through life with much needed grace
No one can put this idea into exile
If it is thrown away
it will extract itself from the pile

Its time has come indeed
Some determined soul will live out its creed
This idea will not be denied
It will live out its existence even though it was criticized

The critics tried to kill the idea,
but it wouldn't die
It crept slowly into existence
as time went by

Destiny and fate
is the origin it was born from
It happened because it is an idea
whose time has come

THE STUFF THAT DREAMS ARE MADE OF

I know the stuff that dreams are made of
It is a motivating force similar to love
You'll sacrifice everything for it
The starts of your dreams are brightly lit

We can envision the accomplishment
of our dreams as clear as day
Determined to make it happen some kind of way

My hopes are built upon my dreams
Daily I swim in its streams

I know that your dreams mean everything to you
To accomplish them
you are doing all that there is to do
A force inside of you motivates you to keep trying
Your dreams become your purpose
and if you aren't living you are dying

The right time is moving too slow
and resources don't come fast enough
Following your dreams can get rough
People who inspire you
proved that dreams can come true
Their actions demonstrate
that you can achieve what you set out to do

Everyday putting in work I be dreaming
Not merely wishing because I know the meaning
What it means to dream
and have to call your own bluff
I have to work hard
to accomplish my dreams and stuff

WE LEARN TO WALK BY FALLING

Before we learned to walk, we first had to crawl
We had to keep our balance
by holding onto the wall
Constantly we fell before we got it right
Still we are trying with all of our might

In life we will walk through many a door
We will not get through
without first falling to the floor
Starting from the bottom
working our way up to the top
Getting tired we rest for a minute to take a stop

After we fall again, we get an energy burst
We jump back to the task feet first
Taking steady steps while we gain our footing
Momentarily conquering the ground
on which our steps is putting

Ten steps forward and falling back five
It's all part of the struggle of being alive
Gaining ground and then losing a little
The finish line shrinks
the distance traveled to a whittle

Walking into success
then falling back into failure again
Knocked down we must stand on our own acumen
Get back up and chase your calling
We learn to walk by falling

EVENTS THAT DEFY EXPLANATION

Things happen that can't be explained
How is this entire universe sustained
Science doesn't explain everything
Like who is the architect of the bird's wing

Every once in awhile something happens
that just blows our mind
Searching for the answers
there is no logical explanation we can find
It is beyond the mind's scope
The intellect reaches for theories
that it fails to grope

Nothing before it seems to resemble
The way it was put together
made it a unique ensemble
A mystery that is so outlandish
Right before your eyes it took a vanish

An event of such stature is very regal
Defying the law but still legal
Outside the boundaries of the ordinary

For such a happening science lacks a category

Look wherever you want
but you will not find a similar genre
This event barks with individuality
Things take place that eclipse our education
Such events defy explanation

TURNING TRAGEDY INTO TRIUMPH

It is possible to find triumph in tragedy
In uncertain moments

you must create an opportunity
You have to pick the pieces up
when it all falls down
Claim your victory and put on your crown

There will be times
that your assets will evaporate like gases
You must become the phoenix
that rises from the ashes
Overcoming your troubles
using your inner prowess
Times like these mandates
moving through life with finesse

When life brings us tragedy, we have to be astute
Digging deep for strength at our root
Life affirming moments challenge us
to be triumphant
Clinging to our dreams
the same way we did as an infant

Certain tragedies make our lives seem unfair

During these hard times
we mustn't give into despair
Even after losing we can come back
to win a victory
Turning the tables as we fight fearlessly

Be resolute in your decision
to survive through adversity
Drink from the river of success
because for it you are thirsty
Tragic situations do take place
that will leave you in a dump
As a survivor
you have to turn tragedy into a triumph

HARD LOVE

At times love is hard
because that is how it is given
The emotions come from
a deep place of feeling
It can be hard when no love is shown to you
One way or another
it is something that we all pursue

Some people love so hard
Others keep those emotions on guard
Love can be a hard thing when you get hurt
You go inside yourself and become an introvert

The pure feeling of love is so sweet
It is healthy for the soul
just as the body needs wheat
Everything about love is noble
Spread all across the world makes it global

We all talk about love so much
The problem is that we don't give it enough
Love is an action word
A feeling that makes you feel superb

When you love hard it shows through action
It is given whole
without pieces falling in a faction
This deep emotion weighs heavy
and it is hard to get above
Unconditionally it is called love

A Ten-Year Long Night
(Not An Overnight Success)

I have been waiting on this night ten long years
Don't think I am sad because I am shedding tears
These are tears of celebration
Finally, I have found success
after a long deliberation

Who knew that one night could be so long
To get to the dawn of success I had to be strong
Now this new day of my life is shining so brightly
My success is not to be taken so lightly

Some people have just heard of me
Little do they know
that this has been a long journey
I have been behind the scenes
struggling for a decade
I worked as an intern before even getting paid

This has been a ten-year apprenticeship
I almost lost it before I could get a grip
I held on against all odds
Kept telling myself that I could
when the critics gave me those nods

It's been a long time coming
Up ahead I must keep running
The finish line is still far ahead out of sight
I still got hard work to do
after resting on this ten-year long night

A FRONT ROW SEAT IN THE THEATER OF HISTORY

We all have a front row seat in the theater of history
Watching it played out like a mystery
Even the audience is a part of the cast
Playing a role that gives the actors a blast

The people are held in suspense
watching the drama on stage
In history there is always some powerful madman
full of rage
He always sets his sights on conquering the world
In the long run history will record
how his evil legacy
began to unfurl

History is so slow to us in the era that we are caught
We sigh at the countless wars that are being fought
This entertainment is so real
The actors are full of zeal

Modern history is being played out
on a regular basis
Look at the curious looks on people's faces
They are all wondering what will happen next
Each actor plays their role to an unwritten text

The scenes are given in parables
within the Holy Scripture
Unbelieving audiences
didn't get the big picture
When the curtains closed, they were napping
and awoke to an unfounded theory
They paid little attention to the show
although they had a front row seat
in the theater of history

THE CREATIVE PROCESS

I was once asked how does an artist undergo
the creative process
Surely it is a miracle
how they perform under duress
They go inside of themselves
and cook up this magic
Pulling off their hat and out comes a rabbit

How does a poet find their muse
Where do they go to find the right words to use
As artists we all got our own creative process
that we undergo
A poet like me just follows
the deepness of my flow

Embryonic ideas start to bubble
in every brain cell

Then the egg of thought is fertilized
with creative gel
Out of your mind burst forth
that idea whose time has come
This is where the creative process is from

On a deeper level
that creative process comes from your soul
A place where all of the right ingredients are in the bowl
You stir them up and get a potent mix
The final product doesn't need a fix

How can you explain the unexplainable
If it isn't genuinely experienced,
the creative process is unattainable
When creative juice flows through you
it doesn't leave a mess
Flowing through your body is this kinetic energy
called the creative process

A LABOR OF LOVE

I love the labor that I do
Although it isn't always the easiest thing to do
I go about my task full of tenacity
Carrying out my duties precisely

My job sometimes keeps me in the throes
I always seem to overcome these woes
There is meaning in our work
No industry can function without a clerk

Some people love doing simple jobs
They label their bosses as snobs
People must find purpose in their occupation
Doing work that gives them an amount of elation

Others love their work so much
that they'll do it for free
Employers don't even have to pay them a fee
There is charity work that involved no profit
Its purpose is to help the less fortunate through
a poverty-stricken grit

Most people labor to earn a wage
Part of mine is writing on this page
Out of everything beyond and above
Writing is my labor of love

Be Humble
While Occupying Your Pride of Place

In life there is a place for pride
Try your best to keep it inside
Life has many roadblocks
upon which we'll stumble
When we get back up and succeed,
we still must be humble

I am not saying that there is anything wrong
with being proud
We just got to quiet ourselves
when we get arrogant and loud
I encourage you to be proud

of what you've achieved
Just don't let your pride have you deceived

Too much pride turns into arrogance
People then begin
to overestimate their importance
Even in our accomplishments
we must display humility
We shouldn't exaggerate our ability

Let's get down off this pedestal before it falls
Humility doesn't mean you shouldn't stand tall
Remember that we were all born
of a humble origin
Arrogant pride is a trait
that we should leave in the margin

Your place in life is only temporary
Pride will leave you at the cemetery
The only reason that we prosper
is due to God's grace
So be humble while occupying

your pride of place

I LOVE THE FEELING OF THE PAGE

The page is more than just another thing to me
Reading and writing gives it a life full of quality
Even when a page is empty
it says something that could be
The embryo of a thought
growing into its infancy

I remember when the teacher gave me
an empty page and told me to write
Trying to compose that first essay
kept me up all night

By the next morning
I had fell in love with what I had wrote
Only to be disappointed when the teacher
corrected my text with an indexed note

Then me and the page
begin to have odds of some sorts
I kept writing what seemed to be
unfinished reports

So, I started reading pages
from another writer's book
It was then at that moment
that the page caught me in its hook

I know that it may sound absurd
But I started falling in love with the written word
As I touch the page, I am overcome with feeling
When it comes to reading, I am more than willing

I am fascinated by the paper and the layout
Technical about how the printer packaged
the book with the writer's clout
Anticipation crowding my mind
as I read the story at the next stage
Oh, how I love the feeling of the page

WHEN COUPLES DECIDE TO CALL IT QUITS

A lot of interrelated things happen
when couples decide to call it quits
Much more drama comes along with it
Some people even lose their identity
Towards life they take on an outlook of apathy

It becomes a greater issue
when children are involved
For their sake, differences need to be solved

Then it is not necessarily about the couple
but about them
From this dilemma
more complicated problems can stem

All over the world couples call it quits everyday
Together they say they couldn't go on that way
Declaring that they'll be better off apart
Somewhere along the way,
they lost each other's heart

Where did the love go
The way that it used to it no longer flows
Some couples tried to make it work again and again
Only to discover that it was best
that they separate in the end

To see two people that were made
for each other break up is tragic

When they were together, they had magic
Friends of spouses don't understand
how they could be involved
in these domestic hits
It seems that everyone is involved
when couples decide to call it quits

ACT ON YOUR INSPIRATION

When you are inspired to do something
don't ignore it
This was your personal solicit
Inspiration just comes out of nowhere
Creative thought and action have to become a pair

We get inspired to do so much

Most of us don't act on it enough
Have you ever been inspired to do something
but failed to carry it out
You thought you couldn't do it
because there was so much doubt

Don't let your inspiration go to waste
Eat it up and don't settle for taste
Once it is digested put it back into the atmosphere
Act out your inspiration without fear

Inspiration comes and it goes
How much of it is wasted nobody knows
We are certain that many people
get inspired but fail to act
Their inspiration was void of tact

Even when you get old
it is difficult to be fully retired
Some new idea will have you so inspired
If you do not carry it out yourself,
pass it on to the next generation
One of your admirers
will act out your inspiration

<u>LIFE IS LIKE A PRACTICE</u>

Life is like a practice
because we are always practicing
Trying to be our best at everything
Keeping in practice our desire to succeed
More practice is something we all need

We seek to put into practice
our well thought out plan
Ignoring our doubts,
we keep telling ourselves we can
With practice we can get better
We will not be hindered by fetter

Exercising our minds
so we can beat the competition
On a quest to place our life in a better condition
Stay in the practice of getting ahead
Make a habit of it instead

Most of our practice is standard,
but it has to be upgraded
The past way of doing things
can get old and faded

Whatever practice you may be in
your life is still your career
Keep trying to put your success into high gear

Practice makes perfect is an old saying
Understand the wisdom that is relaying
You have to practice to get better
after you receive that first strike
Better yet practice at everything
because that is what life is like

IT'S BEEN A LONG TIME COMING

It's been a long time coming
but I still got so far to go
The road ahead must be traveled slow

I've come too far to turn back
Praying to God to give me the strength that I lack

It took me a long time to get here
Moving forward I am leaving the past in the rear
How I made it this far is beyond me
God provided assistance
in those times of uncertainty

There were numerous times
when I thought I couldn't go on
My life was going around in a cyclone
It felt like I was comatose
To death I came so close

I held on and kept going
when life had taken its toll

As a result of the pain my joy had been stole
I have reflected on so much today
Just sitting here realizing that I've come a long way

Reflecting on all the things I've went through
and the places I've been
There was a lot that took place back then
Leaving it all behind
chasing after the future running
It's been a long time coming

LOST BETWEEN THOUGHT AND EXPRESSION

At this moment I am lost

between thought and expression
I know what to say but it won't come out
without guessing
The words are forming too fast in my mind
Hold up let me rewind

How did this thought first come
It blew up in my mind like a bomb
Then thoughts begin exploding everywhere
Tearing apart the stillness that was in the air

Just when I get my thoughts in order,
they continue to evolve
To say what I am feeling, I must gain resolve
What I am thinking is at the tip of my tongue,
but it won't come out
The words are lost in translation
between my mind and my mouth

Sounds begin to rise from my throat
More thoughts drown them out
before I can get them on the boat
Flooding in the sea of my mind with no rescue
I must save my thoughts
before they're lost in the mildew

What we express is a reflection of our thought
In what we are thinking our mind can get caught
So, we must be clear on how we express
what we are thinking
The audience is listening clearly
and they're eyes aren't blinking

EXPERIENCING LIFE

BEYOND YOUR PROBLEMS

It has been said that life
is only what you make it
This is why you have to go through it
using your intelligence and wit
The world is bigger than you
Don't let your life be determined
by what you are going through

There can be a better tomorrow
if you don't get lost in the problems of today
Since being a child, we learned that things
wouldn't always go our way
Problems will present themselves
at every stage of life's journey
These are obstacles that we must overcome
despite the uncertainty

There is so much to experience in life
As long as we don't lose our will
to survive in the strife

Happiness and joy can be experienced
at a moment's notice
We can't let the beauty of life escape our focus

Years from now you'll look back
on this day in curiosity
Your mind will curse your lack of strategy
The world was waiting for you,
but you were caught up in
problems of your own
Opportunities that were once there
are now gone

Do not despair because there will be
many more chances
Only if you stop giving
your problems second glances
The more you look at what's wrong
you can't see what's right
You can't experience life
beyond your problems
if you can't see the light

WORDS ARE LIKE GOLD TO A POET

People like jewels of every kind
But the best one are found in a poet's mind
We dig and dig deep
What we sow is what we reap

A poet's riches is of a different type
Our gold is found in what we write
Words are our riches
The loss of them haunts us like witches

We have an uncanny fascination with words
Our peers call us nerds
While they were wondering
what was at the other end of the rainbow
The poets found their pot of gold
in their next flow

Poets use their words as their currency
Paying dues through the gift of their artistry
Language cashing in its value at a high price
Spending the proceeds to write a literary piece
that is so nice

Great poets have gold buried in their heart
They share their wealth
with the people through their art
For them words never get old
Finding new words to a poet is like finding gold

STUDENTS OF POETRY

We all will always be students of poetry
Trying to figure out which words go in what category
Language will always evolve as it reinvents itself
Even scholars have to constantly search
through the bookshelf

Let's travel back in time
Venture inside the poets mind
Try to figure out how did they come up
with such a rhyme
Why wasn't his classic work
ever published in his prime

Poets forever trying to master the art
We seek to learn so much before we depart
A love of language so close to our heart
With much passion from the start

Poems drawn on your mind like a hieroglyph
Mentally painting a picture of the written script
You spend years studying the stanzas
Digesting it all in your mental canvas

Reading timeless poems that make you reflect
What is the meaning in retrospect
We break down the versus like rocks at the quarry
From the stone age to the present
we remain students of poetry

LIVING TESTIMONY

Every person alive is living their testimony out
Their actions in life say what they are about
People are live testimonies of life's struggles
Bearing many scrapes and bruises
that stand witness to their troubles

Life's testimony is being written daily
Recorded by history with accurate clarity
Books of prophecy
still gives us testimony that is alive
Minds swarm through the contents
like bees on a hive

We are living testimony that our ancestors existed
Our bountiful lifestyle
is because of the famine they resisted

Against tremendous odds they survived
While under enormous pressure
these pioneers thrived

You are living the testimony that is your fate
Destined before your parents became a mate
You are your own witness
Life is an appointment none of us can miss

Our existence on this earth is short
It is a brief amount of time before we depart
We should help future generations succeed
and not leave our legacy lonely
Then after we die, their success will become
a part of our living testimony

USING YOUR GIFT TO HELP OTHERS

A gift is to be given
Yours has no use if you don't share it
while you're living
It was given to you so others you could help
Your gift is not just yours to yourself

You find extra meaning in yourself
when you give of your gift
Especially when it is used to help others get a lift
The good in you reflects
What you both give each other interconnects

Doing all that you can for others
out of goodwill

Your payment is more than the return
on a dollar bill
You get paid with the joy of knowing
that you helped another person out
As a human being, this is what it is all about

Gifts are to be gave
To your wealth you shouldn't be a slave
Like everything else it is to be used
The thought of keeping it to ourselves
must be refused

We all have a gift that we must give
Then you'll experience what it means to live
You took what you had
and give it to help others with
Now that's what I call using your God given gift

DRIVEN BY PROMISE OR PAIN

Striving so hard but what are you driven by
The promise of an abundant future
of the pain of a past cry
To get a better place in life
is what you wish for
Doing all that you can
to pick yourself up off the floor

Thinking back to the days when you were hungry
with your stomach growling
How you went to walking from crawling
In order to succeed you must gain mastery

Making it out of your condition is a necessity

The task before you is so compelling
There are many ways of failing
You must have staying power
The taste of life will get sour

Down the road at every turn is a pitfall
Be strong and focus through it all
Remember the promise that you made
to yourself long ago
You knew that you would endure pain
down the row

The promise of a better future
is your driving force
So, keep traveling down this course
This is what you have to do to make a gain

You are driven by a promise to overcome the pain

TIME IS A GIFT

Besides life, the best gift that we are given is time
We must appreciate every bit of it even
when we aren't in our prime
Although every part of life is not so fantastic
Somehow you should try to be enthusiastic

Don't waste your time in a somber
You never know when heaven may call your number
Jog through life with the pace of a runner
Hitting your stride as you turn the corner

Time shouldn't be wasted in inactivity
Each day must be used critically
Its importance is of the utmost
Treat with courtesy this host

The time that we have on this earth
is a precious commodity
A lot of things happen to us during this odyssey
Take advantage of the time that you are given
Don't waste away the life that you're living

How will you spend your time today
What will you do as the seconds, minutes,
and hours tick away
When tragedy strikes and your spirits need a lift
Just remind yourself that time is a gift

FROM DEPRESSION CAN COME THE GREATEST ART

Much of our greatest art
was created out of depression
You'll never believe
what they were going through in that session
Some of these artists
were even on the verge of suicide
Through their art they were able to feel
a sense of pride

History has recorded some of the depression
they were going through
Despite their troubled lives, their art remained true
Saddened by life but they found contentment
in their artform
Their majestic creations were outside the norm

A lot of artists today are depressed
Judging by their works, you'd never had guessed
We all know depression firsthand
How such brilliant artistry resulted
from it is hard to understand

It is unimaginable that a bout of depression
was at the center of this masterpiece
In the midst of sadness
their artistic creativity didn't cease
Locked in a mode of depression
they still have artistic freedom
Escaping into their art to seek refuge

in their personal kingdom

Depression can even
become an artist inspiration
To forget their problems,
they get lost in the work and focus
with absolute dedication
It's ironic that the genius we see coming
from artist isn't always because they're smart
From depression
came some of the world's greatest art

PAIN HAS A PURPOSE

Pain is something that we all try to stay away from
No matter which way it comes
As a part of life it will always be there
I know it doesn't always seem fair

Insight will allow us to see

that pain has a purpose to serve
To endure it we have to get up our nerve
Pain is a part of this life we live
It is something that we take and give

Take the pain
and let it make you stronger
Not finding purpose in it
only makes you suffer longer
The pain that you are enduring
probably isn't your fault
Find divine meaning in it
because it does no good to revolt

It doesn't feel good to hurt
Yet we have done our share of dirt
In our wrongdoing we hurt someone else also
What we did struck a bruise to their ego

Pain comes and it quickens that pulse
You've got to feel it
but to find no meaning in it is false
When you get hurt don't let it be in vain
You must find a purpose in your pain

<u>OUT OF BODY EXPERIENCES</u>

Our souls speak of a connection
far wiser than our years
At times we have experiences
that are misunderstood by peers

With them, we may have been physically present
Yet of their sayings, we were negligent

To them we may as well have been on Mars
Our eyes were lost in the stars
It seemed that we have seen a ghost
by the look on our face
We were mentally in outer space

Experiences take place within our body
that we can't explain
What happened
seemed beyond the perimeter of our brain
Science is baffled by the anatomy
In its research, it is an inconclusive analogy

None of us are exempt
Out of body experiences
are not something that we can tempt

They just happen out of nowhere
It can be quite a scare

This is not something that researchers can mimic
What I am writing about is not a gimmick
An experience that defies the laws of biology
Something happens inside of you,
but it seems outside of your body

THE PRODUCTION OF THE POEM

First allow the poem to speak to you
even before the words form

Be original and write something
outside of the norm
Listen to the sound in your mind
as the poem is in produce
Let the rhythm of the words flow
through your creative juice

Clear the static from the speaker of your mind
Then new rhythms you will begin to find
The drumbeat of your heart will guide your flow
Use the instrumentals of your soul
to create the tempo

Intuitively the poem will begin to talk to you
Just do what it tells you to do
Write from a place deep down inside your depth
Make sure that it is heartfelt

Get in sync with the audience

as they absorb the energy from the poetry
Go inside their mind to discover
what they find unique about your story

Review what you've wrote
and become the listener
The feedback from your gut
has to be louder than a whisper

Always challenge yourself to be better
on the next poem that you engineer
Become one with the fans
as they give you a round of applause and cheer
Helping them to feel empowered
becomes your inspiration
After the curtains close
listen to them give you a standing ovation

PRESERVATION OF THE FAMILY STRUCTURE

The structure of the family we must preserve
Keeping it together with verve
This is the mainstay of society
Order revolves around family

In modern times the family structure
has been deteriorating
All because of the actions
in which its members are participating
The unit of family must not fall apart
Let's correct its deficiencies from the heart

The family structure has to regain its threshold
We can't let it fold
All of us have to keep it together
Wear it on our back with the warmth of leather

Without a strong foundation the structure will fall
The loss of family causes us to lose it all
For this reason we've got to preserve it at all cost
If we don't this will be our greatest loss

Keeping the family structure tight is top priority
Over every other issue this one takes seniority
Family is at the center piece of every nation
Its structure must undergo preservation

A STUDENT OF GREAT THINKERS

After studying his style,
I can see that he is a student
of those who were great
This is what his method of operation
seems to indicate
I first noticed the books that he read
In the direction he is headed, this gives him a lead

Staying abreast of progress of people like him
has motivated me
They act out their ambitions with integrity
I no longer wonder why they study thinkers
who had a great reputation
These role models of theirs gave them inspiration

Every great thinker is a student of those
who came before them
From their archives
they've extracted some lyrical gem

Listen to that great thinker
when he or she is at the pulpit
There may be an area of your life
that their logic may fit

Thought provoking statements
are associated with these great teachers
History has recorded them as writers, politicians,
and leaders
Let's not exclude those great thinkers
who were ordinary laymen
People blessed of refined acumen

Great thinkers are those historic figures
we learn from
Much wisdom can even be acquired through a bum
Not learning from their lessons
caused their life to go down like a sinker
Like us they too are students of a great thinker

Rising to The Challenge

From the moment that you were born
life was waiting to challenge you
At every opportunity,
it will present one that's new
When the challenge presents itself,
you must rise to it
Now is not the time to quit

Each day a new challenge will arise
Don't let this be a surprise
When it comes it has to be dealt with
Iron out your challenges
with the professionalism of a blacksmith

Go up against the challenge with fortitude
Bring down your apprehension with crude
Face the challenge head on
Put your body in a protective zone

Meet the challenge as it is presented
Don't be the one who relented
When you fall find your footing again
Rise up to the challenge and try to win

Even if you lose, at least you can say you tried
Avoiding a challenge
only causes it to be multiplied
As the punches of life knock you down,
find your balance
Get back up and rise to the challenge

FAITH WITHOUT WORDS

Faith without works will get you no where
Without taking a step you can't climb the stair
God commanded you to believe
Working is not something
from which He gives us a relieve

Blind faith makes no sense
Ignorance of your own beliefs is no defense
Faith is stronger than reason, but reason
is what you put your faith in
Don't blindly follow your next of kin

It is only through solid investigation and research
that faith is justified
Then deep in your soul is the place it must reside
Once it is established,
don't let the world shake your faith

Hold on to it until your death date

With faith comes the workings
that coincide with your belief
It was only hard work and experience
that allowed him to become a chief
Our faith is something that we put work in for
Without effort we can't wait on a miracle
to walk through the door

After you pray,
let faith be the anchor your hopes hang upon
While you wait, work has to be done
True belief doesn't promise artificial perks
Faith alone profits us nothing without works

BLESSED WITH A BURDEN

It weighed heavy on me
and this burden I didn't want to carry
I sought divine help in a hurry
A wise man said that God doesn't give us a burden
that we can't bear
I looked at him with a confused stare

Why was this burden given to me
I could have dealt with something else
a little more easy
He told me,
that is exactly why God gave you this one
There is wisdom in what He has done

I pondered on what he said

and it began to make sense
Right then at that moment
my mind stopped being tense

I realized it wasn't all about me,
but about helping other people
Part of my burden
is battling against my own inner evil

What we look at as a burden
can turn out to be a blessing
Pay close attention to the problems
we are addressing
Turn it around and put it in your favor
Find the solution and don't put it off on a waiver

At first, this burden used to have me stressed
Still I have to thank God because I am blessed

Carrying it will get difficult I am certain
Either way I am blessed with a burden

MAKING A WAY OUT OF NO WAY

She was told that there was no way
that she could make it on her own
A fifteen-year-old single parent who left home
I saw my mother make a way
when there was none
During trying times,
she said all you gotta do is believe son

When the four walls of life closed in on us,
she created a new door
Giving us the warmth of love when
we couldn't afford heat because we were poor
Nights when there was no food,

- 86 -

she filled our bellies with the hope of tomorrow
We experienced inner joy
even in the midst of our sorrow

From her example, I believe I can make it
though they said I can't
I refuse to give into this complaint

People criticize, but I can hear my mother
saying forget what they say
This was a piece of advice
she gave her children before she passed away

All I keep telling myself is that
I have to make it no matter what
Give life my best effort from the gut
Another old saying declares

that if there is a will there is a way
Look to tomorrow
despite the desperateness of today

There is a way if we keep searching
Continuing to look even when life is lurching
The future is ours for the taking
Let there be no way
that we will not find a way of making

A POET'S AFTERTHOUGHT

A poet's afterthought never seems to end
We always have a new message to send
Death doesn't even make our afterthoughts final
Posthumous works
will continue to appear on vinyl

We use verses to make our message fit
Afterward we edit to make sure it's legit
The critics may not like our final draft
In their opinion we haven't perfected the craft

If it weren't for the artist,
then the critic wouldn't exist
Their outrageous analysis of our works
often end balled up in our fist
Postmortem we critique our own work
Writing to please the critics will drive you berserk

Every poet knows that there is room
for improvement
The evolution of language
is a continuous movement
So, we take our part in this literary revolution
Changing the course of the world
through a written solution

Poets are often overcome with fresh inspiration
We write or speak it for the people

with no hesitation
In the web of creativity, we are forever caught
So, read on as you absorb a poet's afterthought

EXPERIENCE IS THE BEST TEACHER

We learn from the experiences that we go through
They teach us what and what not to do
Experience warns us not to repeat
the past mistakes that we've made
Such hard-learned lessons aren't likely to fade

Once we've experienced something,
we know that thing firsthand
For what we believe in, we must take a stand

Going into every situation realizing
what experience has taught us
Logically putting forth our arguments
without making an unnecessary fuss

By going through it we know what to avoid
This does not mean that we should be paranoid
We just can't be naive
In the fight for survival
you have to bob and weave

Listen to your intuition and sensibility
Don't get caught up in complacency
Analyze the situation critically
Use your acquired experience and be savvy

What we may go through in the future
is full of uncertainty
When things don't go as we planned,

we must act strategically
Most of our life lessons
are not learned from a preacher
Experience is the best teacher

IN A HURRY TO FINISH

I am in a hurry to get through
So many things that I got to do
I refuse to rush and be sloppy
If I do, I'll have to redo it over in a copy

I'm just ready to get it over with
Trying to solve this myth

When you're almost through
you can't wait till it ends
Afterwards taking a rest
is how you make amends

Impatient as I get this task complete
I have a deadline to meet
The finish-line is in sight
Still I have to take my time and do it right

The end can take the longest
That's when the anticipation
comes on the strongest
At this time,
you can't wait to finish what you're doing
In the pot of your mind

future activities are brewing

How much longer will it take is what you ask
It's about time to complete this task
Later I'll have to take a little time to replenish
Right now, I am in a hurry to finish

THE ANSWER IS IN THE QUESTION

Listen closely to the question
and there you will have the answer
Falling in line like the camper
You have to see that the forest
can't exist without the trees

Find solid ground
while walking through the leaves

Why do you ask what you should know already
During the test, keep your mind steady
To find the answer, search your memory
and your brain will spark a fuse
Study the book and ponder on what you pursue

Step out of the square of mediocrity
and your circle of thought will expand
Approach the debate with the spirit of a firebrand
Not one who causes trouble
but the one who challenges the status quo
Prove to the powers that be that they are wrong
in what they think they know

I told you before to never judge
a book by its cover
Inside the pages is where the answers hover
Let the truth found in the books be your haven

Make an impact and be a maven

Don't doubt yourself when you are able
Seek for truth in your mental stable
The teacher must quiet the classroom
and silence the fussing
Tell the students
that the answer is in the question

NOW I KNOW WHY THE BEST THINGS ARE FREE

The best things in life don't cost a thing
Look inside yourself and see that love is king
There are some things that can't be paid for

Precious gifts that can't be bought at the store

Nature isn't supposed to come with a price tag
Love isn't found in a brown paper bag
God has given mankind
the best gifts free of charge
The quantities come small and large

Talent is instilled in us when we were born
Our outlook on life need not be forlorn
Money can't buy us everything that we need
We must free ourselves from our own greed

Human companionship is given to us naturally
We all share our humanity
There is nothing better than can be given
Appreciating life is a goal
to which we should all be driven

As I feel love, I know it can't be bought

It is something that doesn't cost
Life's greatest gifts don't cost a fee
Now you should know
why the best things in life are free

ORDINARY PEOPLE WITH EXTRAORDINARY TALENT

Everyday we meet ordinary people

who have talent that is extraordinary
Often, we place people in the same category
Each one of us have something about us
that is unique
Although other things about us
may be normal and bleak

A radiance shines from some souls
that seems to captivate
Something about a certain persona
that causes it to radiate
Shining forth a light from their interior
that make them sparken
Even on gloomy days,
their disposition doesn't darken

An everyday person with an additional quality
that seems animated
A natural gift that divine powers
must have orchestrated

Extraordinary in that they have a talent
that seems like an extra gift

Additional components
that causes personality shift

They are so regular
when they are around you and me
Yet there is a greatness flowing
from their humanity
It lightens their countenance up like a flint
The brightness shines too hard
to hide behind tint

Their talent dresses their personality up
like a pageantry
With a personal signature that verifies
its authenticity
Brilliance dominates this certain characteristic
These are just ordinary people
with a talent that is so prolific

WRITING IS LIKE BUILDING A HOUSE

Writing is like building a house
in that you start from the ground up
Laying the foundation
so the structure won't be corrupt
The original concept of the story
is like the basement
Setting the stage for the rooms
as you lay down the pavement

Starting at the floor of your mind
you build with raw material
Walling off your thoughts
with an interior design that is imperial
Installing words that flow through the hallways
of your paragraphs like electricity
Editing the original piece leaves you plumbing
through the sentence with a dictionary

You must stay creative
while carving out your own niche
Building a house that will make
the reader feel rich

In every room, they get a visual interchange
between literature and art
Just reading what is in your personal library
makes them feel smart

Now that the house is complete,
it is ready to be occupied
Secret spots throughout
where the imagination can hide
There is plenty of room for the curiosity
of the guest
When they study the interior,
they see that the architect gave his best

Characters of the story are furniture
that give the house its decoration
Splendid sculptures
that gain the readers' admiration

There are exquisite pieces
hanging from the ceiling
Every time you write a story
it is a house that you are building

MAKE HISTORY WHILE REMAKING YOURSELF

There is something about yourself
that you desire to change
While you are doing this,
you must expand your range
Try to do something
that has never been done before
Dig deeper than the surface and get to the core

Envision yourself doing something paramount
Multiply your accomplishments
but don't keep count

Symbolically climb mountains
that only you can reach the peak
Capitalize off that character trait
that makes you unique

As you remake yourself,
don't forget about the picture that's bigger

This transformation will be more difficult
than you first begin to figure

Fly to new heights as you reach your zenith
Go the distance as if your life depended on it

Tighten up those lose strings in your life
like a braid
Broaden the scope beyond yourself
because history had to be made
Strive to becomes greater than your hero
Be the star of your own show

Ignore the critics when they are being cynical
Expect them to doubt your success
as you reach your pinnacle
There is so much at stake
Redo yourself while history is on the make

THE WHOLE IS GREATER
THAN THE SUM OF ITS PARTS

Without its parts nothing can be whole
Therefore, each part of a thing
plays an important role
Not so important as to equal the sum
of all the other pieces
If one part is left out, then production ceases

The whole means everything and all
Unity keeps it together,
but division causes it to fall
In life, the people are the parts of an organization
or a company
The different skills that they possess
creates a needed diversity

Each person has some unique skill

that they bring
Still they are not more important
than the whole thing

As long as people realize this,
the operation flows smoothly
Problems start when individuals lack ingenuity

Individuality stands out
through hard work and progress
Personal achievement
is what such accomplishments stress
The person is only a part of
what makes a thing complete
A single body within the entire fleet

Add up the parts and you get the full value
All the ingredients must be included
to make the human that's you
There can be no life
if blood doesn't pump through our hearts
The whole of the body

is greater than the sum of its parts

BEFORE MY PEN REST

Before I rest my pen,
there is something I'd like to declare
I have a pen that takes flight and stays in the air
In my mind I keep drifting off into this poetic zone
Language just won't leave me alone

Versus form in my head even when I am thinking
of something totally unrelated
I was trying to do something else
and my pen could have waited
Impatiently it took over my schedule
and started writing
Expressing what a deeper part of me was reciting

My pen doesn't seem to want to take a break
True to form,

I am a lyricist with a point to make
It's crazy that my pen appears
to have a mind of its own
Poetry flowing so deep in me
that I can feel it in my bone

Just when I take a hiatus from writing,
some new ideas will form
My persistent pen insisted that I write this poem
Words and me have a special connection
In recording what's on my mind, my pen refuses
to make a defection

Only when I sleep does my pen sit idly by
I guess it will finally rest when I die
When I write I give my best
I just wanted you to know this before my pen rest

HOPING THE SKY TELLS ME A STORY

As I walk or sit in distress,
I look towards the sky
hoping it will tell me a story
When I look at the world,
I see no more glory
I look up to see the beauty of the earth
The calmness of the sky
always suppresses my hurt

I was once told that the sky has no limits
To its inhabitants this is a privilege
When I look up at the sun,
I know that millions occupy the same sight
It gives the world its needed light

The sky is full of so many gracious things
What I love about it most is when
the birds fly and spread their wings
I love the sky at day and at night
It lets me know that everything
is going to be alright

The sky knows my every secret
I don't mind
because in its depths it will keep it

Me and the sky
has shared so many precious moments
It will always be my place of refuge
when I can't win over my opponents

Sometimes I feel that the sky is mine,
but yet it belongs to none but one
We all know this after everything is said and done
Tell me a story oh sky
Please answer my questions and tell me why

The sky holds the key to many a mystery
It has always been a witness
to this world's history
When loneliness overwhelms me
getting rid of it is mandatory
I always look for the sky to tell me a story.

HAVE YOU EVER NEEDED
SOMETHING SO BAD

Have you ever needed something so bad
Something that you've always wanted
but never had
Or you may have had it before
but can't get to it at this time
You want it so bad
that it feels like your about to lose your mind

Do you crave for something or someone
Without that particular things or person,
you feel like you just want to run

Run to a place
where you will find them residing
With them in your arms
there will be no need in hiding

There is something that you want but can't get
Or is it a special someone that you want to be with
This is a person that you will do anything for
In your heart, they are at the core

Is it peace that you crave
Are you tired of being surrounded
by madness and rage
Have you ever just wanted to get away
Do you wish that it was in paradise that you lay

When you get close
You can taste it the most
Then you'll see something else
that you think will make you glad
It'll just be another one of those things

that you want so bad

ANGER IS THE RESPONSE TO INJUSTICE

Anger is the response to any felt injustice
When we feel that we have been treated unjustly
anger will surface
Anger will cause us to justify our actions
when we do something wrong
We sometimes react in a destructive way
when our anger comes on strong

We have to stop letting anger blind us
Controlling our anger

is something that we must not fail to discuss
Often, we make the mistake
of taking our anger out on others
We often release our anger
under false disguises and covers

Anger is at the root of many an emotion
We can't escape our problems
through a substance illusional potion

We have to start dealing
with the root of our anger
If we don't we will always be in danger

We must not let our anger control our lives
If we do we will make mistakes
that we come to despise
When we reach this apex
we must face our anger head on

Letting anger dictate our lives
is something that we can't condone

Anger will always affect the relationships
in our lives in some way
So, we must know that unconsciously
hurting people will ruin our day
Anger is the response to any form of injustice
We must remember that behind our angry actions
there is a consequence

MY MIND IS LIKE A RIOT IN THE MORNING

I wake up in the morning
tired from a long night
Sleep is calling me, but the energy circulating
in my mind makes it a losing fight
My brain is restless with endless thoughts
of the upcoming day
I want to doze back off,
but countless mental chatter

keeps getting in the way

My mind is just all over the place
Reminding me of memories of yesterday
that I am trying to erase
Thought after thought busting windows
and looting my prefrontal cortex
A little nod here and there gets overrun
with mental alarms going off in the index

Tranquility in the morning
is something that I can't keep
Thoughts racing through my mind
preventing me from going back to sleep

Mental sirens ringing me back awake
Dozing off my mind
gets looted continuously without a break

Laying here half asleep
my mind keeps pondering over many things
All the while replaying the events
from last night's dreams
I just need a few more hours to rest
Early in the morning my mental creativity
is at its best

After thirty minutes or so
I realize that I can't sleep through a riot
All I wanted was some peace and quiet
Pulling myself out of bed to start a new day
with a mental warning
I start off full of energy
because my mind is like a riot in the morning

WHEN THE WORLD STOPPED CARING

I wonder when the world stopped caring last night
How did we get authority
to make a wrong into a right
Here we are living in a time of adultery, mischief,
and schemes
My elders tell me it isn't as bad as it seems

When the human nature became filled
with greed, lust, and envy
The world stopped caring
and we became our own worst enemy
We live in a time where so many people
have stopped caring
Even mothers with their own kids
have stopped sharing

Society provides an atmosphere where every
man, woman, and child are for themselves
It says be successful and forget everyone else
We blame politicians, but we buy the dreams they sell

When they get elected into office,
we are disappointed as they fail

So many religious sects wonder why
the world stopped caring last night

Why was that innocent man killed
when he tried to break up that fight
They wonder why the world closes its ears
when they try to deliver God's Word
What part of their message was even heard

SCARED TO LOSE

Why are we so scared to lose
How come when we are not victorious,
we catch the blues
Having fun isn't all about winning

If the opposite is your theory,
you forsake the fun in the beginning

Everyone wants to win
but you have to pay your dues
You can't be scared to lose
Everyone seeks to be the best in what they do
I must remember that there's always somebody
better than you

The three options of any game are
win, lose, or draw
Every time you lose,
you can't consider it as a flaw
Winning can become a mad obsession
If you fail, you may lose a valuable possession

Every quest that you wish to conquer in life
is a challenge
Desiring to win everything

can keep your true focus off balance
So be a good sport in whatever you do
Understand that there are times when you will lose

Some people lie and cheat to win
But still lose in the end
So, don't be afraid to lose in some of the ventures
that you pursue in life
Just be pleased that you went out with a fight

What if you had nothing to lose
and everything to gain
If you lost everything how would you maintain
When you take a chance
it's good to think before you choose
You cannot always win so do not be scared to lose

THE CHANCES THAT WE TAKE

Life's consequences comes as a result
of the chances that we take

The situations that we find ourselves in
are because of the decisions we make
We take chances
with life's everyday operations
Without surely knowing
the outcome of these situations

Some say that taking chances
is always mandatory in life
Even though some of these chances are not even right
With every new device made today
was first a chance that was took
One cannot create without taking a second look

Some of the chances that we take
are novel while others are suicidal
Uncertain gambles become our most intimate rival

Will you continue to take uncertain chances

with the life you live
Not knowing the end results of this
So before you take the last dance
Make sure that you have selected
a desired partner and not one taken on a chance

EVEN THOUGH IT SEEMS HOPELESS

You must keep trying
even though it may seem hopeless
You can't let hard times make you lose focus
After all the failures there is still hope
When you slip hold on tighter to the rope

They say that desperate times
call for desperate measures
We must know that patience
is a dominate treasure
Meaning that things are not going to get better
at your say so
Good things does come
to those who wait though

We all know that many wonder
why times are so bad
They wonder what happened
to the days when they were glad

It seems that those days are not lost and gone
Faith will let them know
that they are not far from home

How hopeless can the times that we live in be
All I know is that things are going to get better
for you and for me
The only weapon I know
to fight hopelessness with is faith
I see a way to light beyond the darkness
of this present state

Belief in better times
is what keeps me a sane mind
I know that brighter times
aren't just lost and behind
Better days lie ahead in these times
of desperation if we do not lose focus
In time it will get better even though right now
it seems to be hopeless

TRYING TO MAINTAIN

I am up under so much pressure
and trying to maintain
It is only the faith that I got in better times
that keeps me sane
I don't know how I deal with all this pain
I'm just trying to make it
not even searching for fortune and fame

I'm just trying to maintain a steady life
One in which I will have no problem
feeling my kids and wife
Slowly I am learning to maintain at a steady pace
Dealing with my problems face to face
I face another new problem everyday
As I've matured, I now understand that life
will continue on this way

I must continue to maintain
in everything that I pursue
Keeping my head above water
is something I must do
In due time I will possess the needed clue
Meanwhile I must hold my life
together like glue

Although the world isn't the same
I can't let it get me down
to the point of becoming insane
I always got to keep trying to maintain

CARRYING THE WORLD ON MY SHOULDER

A drunk old man said
"young man take the world off your shoulder"
He told me that I was carrying
too heavy a boulder
I looked to him and smirked
He said: "don't try to fool me shorty,
I been there, and I know it hurt"

The old man told me I was too young
to be mad at the world
When he told me, my lips curled
He said: "son take the frown off your face
cause when I was young, I didn't want to listen."
That's why he is sitting here
trying to solve his problems with a bottle of gin

My associates said,
"Man forget what that old fool is talking about"
Then the man ceased to talk and began to shout

As my comrades walked away,
me and the old man at the curb remained
He said being angry all the time
ain't gonna change a thang

He told me to take the whole world
off of my shoulder
Because everyday this world gets colder
He told me that I didn't need to find the answer
to every question
So I should quit
all this complaining and fussing

Old man told me that I was carrying too much weight
He told me to show love
and stop expressing so much hate
He told me not to let the world bring me down
Trouble is what makes it go round

He said that he survived because he is a fighter

He said that when I walked away
my burden would be much lighter
He told me to put this lesson in my life's folder
And to take the weight of the world up off my shoulder

STRESSING AND DEPRESSING

Sometimes life can have you depressed
With so much pain and confusion in your inner chest
You'll wonder how to deal with all the stress
This is just all a part of you reaching your quest

Life isn't easy for anyone
Everybody undergoes boredom
before they find fun
You are not the only one
who feels like the world is closing in on you
We all find ourselves sometimes
not knowing what to do

It's hard to get by without nothing
But you will not always be suffering
Sometimes it feels that you are stuck
in the same chapter

Seeming to forever be caught in a rapture

There's many a productive way
to deal with stress
During distressful times you have to produce
your strength at its best

That's the only way that you'll make it
You have to struggle to be organized
when things get hectic

We have to remember
that God hasn't forgot about us
When we keep faith, He'll always give us a plus
He foretold us that life
will sometimes be depressing
Through good and bad times
praise to Him is what we need to be stressing

Nobody Is Going To
Take Care of You Like You

Nobody is going to take care of you
like you take care of yourself
So how come some of us
keep depending on somebody else
We have to be more independent
and self-motivated
Afterwards, we will know that
this is the best way to make it

Sometimes we all need somebody to lean on
At the same time,
we have to face certain problems on our own
There will not always be a person around to help you
That's when you have to do for yourself

the best that you can do

People feel much better
when they stand on their own
That's a strong foundation towards establishing
an independent home

Independence in a person's character is rewarding
As a result, things you couldn't buy at first
you will find yourself affording

Some of us have to take care of others
While others are dependent
upon sisters and brothers
We have to get out and do for us
Or else we will go without this, that, and thus

No one is going to take care of you like you will
Being independent is a great way to feel
We must all learn to depend on ourselves
No one will take care of you

like you will take care of yourself

SOMEONE TO TALK TO

When you need someone to talk to
I will be there to listen to you
There is nothing to fear
Your words are safe in my ear

Even when you get weak
Or just find it hard to speak
I can still understand what you are trying to say
The words are written all over your face

If you have been holding something in
and you need to let it out
Express yourself and let me know

what you are talking about
I will hear your every word
Nothing coming out of your mouth
will go unheard

I will be open-minded
My opinions will not be one-sided
I feel your story just as I feel mine
Empathy for your struggle is what I find

Words unspoken are still felt
I understand where your thoughts are at
Maybe I have been there a time or two
If not, I will go on that journey with you

You don't have to keep everything inside
In me you can confide

When no one seems to understand you
I am someone you can talk to

<u>MY FUTURE IS SO HARD TO SEE</u>

Sometimes my future is so hard to see
At times I wonder what my future holds for me
My past makes me wonder
if there's a better tomorrow
When I think about my future,
I know it's something I'll have to borrow

I know I possess the talent to make my future great
But to spend my future incarcerated
in something I will hate
There is no way that I am giving up

And I know my future depends on
more than just luck

I know my future consists of
pain, pleasure, and grief
I wish my future was simple
as a meal one would eat
But my future holds many a complication
My future is an unknown situation

I wonder if my future
is my vision in my dreams
Will I ever see what my future means
Only God has the answers
to the questions that I ask
He knows I lived my life too fast

My faith makes me believe in the unseen
My future consist of so many things
Whether I be in heaven or on earth

One day my body will be in the dirt

Life goes on no matter where I be
God is the Greatest and I shall praise thee
Without Him I have no future to see

HOW FAR CAN A MINORITY GO UNDER

In time I have sat and wondered
how far can a minority go under
I have come to many concrete solutions
to putting an end to this everlasting slumber
Being a minority and thinking there is no hope is
a misunderstood confusion
In every inhumane situation
we encounter there is a solution

Minorities consist of the majority
of the earth's population
If we unite, we can overcome
our hazardous situation
We have to take over the politician machine
and elect candidates who are truly in popularity
This way the government will be for the people
by the people since we are the real majority

Minority groups are kept down
by mass overhead oppression
Many minority businessmen went bankrupt
after every bank gave their loan a rejection

In order for us minorities to succeed
We must unite and make our factories
to fulfill our everyday need

If us minorities do not unite,
we will continue to be oppressed
The more power we give our oppressors
they remain power obsessed
One race of minorities should not look down

on another minority group
Having the smallest notion
that you are better than them is untrue

The oppressors most successful tactic
is to keep us in disunity
It is up to us to hold them accountable
and dismantle their impunity
The truth of this poem can save minorities
who suffer billions by the number
I ask you again, how far can a minority go under

WE ALL HAVE OUR CHANCE TO SHINE

We all will have our chance to shine
Our talents will get better with time
We are all unique in one way or another
After we fail
there's some way that we can recover

We will get our chance in the spotlight

Some of us will not take advantage of this
but others might
Sometimes it seems like you will never make it
You will have to put in a lot of work
without making a profit

If you ever want to really shine
you will have to pay your dues
If you quit nobody will lose out but you
Your works may not be good enough
for someone else
If you keep trying eventually,
you'll find business at the right address

Shining requires possessing a special gift
One in which every time it's displayed it is given a lift
Shining also requires having skill
Which is given its strength from your own will

Others in your field may shine better than you

But you will receive notice
as long as you are good at what you do
It is good to be in a class of your own
Always coming with originality in your tone

Whatever it is that you do you can one day succeed
You have to be patient
and you cannot be motivated by greed
If you keep the work that you do first at mind
You will eventually get your chance to shine

POETRY IS THE SOUL OF A PERSON SPEAKING

Poetry is a vehicle that one uses to expose
the depths of their soul
It allows them to tell stories
in a way that they never could have told
Through poetic revelation

the most controversial things
are simply explained
The soul is complex,
but it can also be simple and plain

Since poetry is always written directly or indirectly
in a soulful way
It coincides with a person's soulful feelings
just as night turns into day
Let your soul flow and write for you
Words will begin to come forth
expressing soul sentiments so true

A friend once told me
that poetry is the soul of a person speaking out
So now I write this poem to explain exactly
what she is talking about

Poetry is a substantial way for a person
to let their soul communicate
It permits a person to say something
in way that they wouldn't face to face

The contents of a poem can be wrote
through a spiritual or everyday experience
It depends on the source of the person's influence
People come from different backgrounds
and live different lifestyles
This is why poetry is used distinctively
and has a distinct profile

A poem explains a person's message
in a unique fashion
Verses of a poem come from the soul
so therefore, they are full of passion
So, if you ever want to say something
that your mouth is keeping
Write a poem because poetry is the soul
of a person speaking

SITUATIONS AND CIRCUMSTANCES

A situation comes about from a circumstance
To escape the circumstances, we take chances
There is no limit to the situations

that one may find themselves in
It's good to seek out better atmospheres
every now and then

A situation can be defined as a state of affairs
It is not singular but often comes in pairs
One must make of a situation what it is
No matter how bad it may be,
you must make the best of this

A circumstance can be defined
as conditions attending an event
There are some circumstances
that we cannot prevent
Some things are just ordained
Meaning that there is some situations
and circumstances that we can't change

A situation is a position of the office
or job in which you hold

At odd times this can leave you trapped
in a dark spot in the cold
Don't let the situation that you are in
determine your fate
Better things come
to those who work hard and wait

Do not let the circumstances that you are under
control your destiny
You and the people who look down on you
are in an unspoken rivalry
Life is not all about taking chances
So, find ways to better your own situation
and circumstances

<u>IT'S TIME TO SEE WHAT YOU'VE BEEN MISSING</u>

It is time to see what you have been missing

Open your ears and listen
You have to start being open minded
Then you will realize that
to a lot of good things you've been blinded

Life has many adventures for you to explore
You just have to set your focus
toward a higher score
Aren't you tired of traveling the same circles
round and round
Seeing the same sights
and hearing the same sounds
It is time to be a part of new things
Put into your reality your most potent dreams

It is a lot more to the world than you know
Let back the curtains and look at the show
There is plenty of new sights for you to see
The universe is an ever-expanding monopoly

It is not always good to be closed in
Get out and meet new friends
The world has a lot to offer you
There are things that you have to get out and pursue

It is time for you to put on a new smile
Get out and explore the world for awhile
Life keeps passing you by while time is steadily ticking
You need to get out into the world
and see what you have been missing

I WAS BORN BY THAT RIVER

Pain surfaced that river that I was born by
There was no father at my mother's side
I guess he didn't care rather I was born or either died
He was somewhere doing drugs
getting himself high

So when I say that I was born by that river
The contents of this poem are
what I want you to remember
I was born on a freezing day in the month of January
Even though my mother needed help
she found no place of sanctuary

I was born by that riverbank
The pain that my mother underwent is a shame
I indeed was born by that river
Some of the harsh things that were said
about my mother
will make you shiver

When I tell you, I was born by that river,
do you truly understand what I say
My mother and I shed so many tears
we made a river that day

There were tears of joy and tears of sorry
My mother wondered
how she was going to get by tomorrow

People I was born by that riverbed
It is only the charity of my mother's meager
wealth that kept me fed
Times seemed to stay hand
With my mama and daddy forever apart

No matter how high the water in the river got
My mama always managed to keep food in our pot
I wasn't born with a spoon of silver
I was born by that river

Other Books to Read

By: Bobby Bostic

Dear Mama: The Life and

Struggles of a Single Mother

Generation Misunderstood:

Generation Next

Time

Endless Moments

In Prison

Mental Jewelry:

Wear It on Your Brain

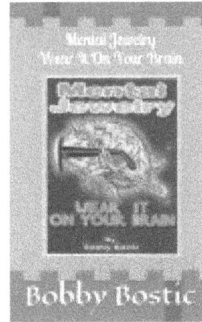

When Life Gives You lemons:

Make Lemonade

Life Goes on Inside Prison

Also look for future books, products,

and merchandise by Bobby Bostic.